SHELLY Goes to the BANK

Allison Martin & Kentrell Martin

The Shelly's Adventures Series

Shelly Goes to the Bank by Allison Martin and Kentrell Martin

Copyright © 2017 by Kentrell Martin
All rights reserved. No part of this publication may be reproduced, copied, or stored in a retrieval system, or transmitted in any form or by any means, electronic, mechanical, photocopying, recording, or in any way for any reason, without the written permission of the publisher.

ISBN (hardcover): 978-0-9851845-8-2
ISBN (softcover): 978-0-9851845-7-5
ISBN (ebook): 978-0-9851845-9-9
Library of Congress Control Number: 2017907348

Book design by Jill Ronsley, suneditwrite.com
Illustrations by Nguyen Minh Duc
Vector icons in this book designed by Freepik, flaticon.com

Published by Shelly's Adventures LLC
PO Box 2632, Land O Lakes, Fl 34639 USA
www.shellysadventuresllc.com

10 9 8 7 6 5 4 3 2 1

Printed and bound in the USA

Shelly's Adventures LLC was created to provide children and their parents with reading material that teaches American Sign Language. Shelly's Adventures LLC produces materials that make signing fun for kids, parents and teachers.

 https://www.facebook.com/ShellysAdventures

 https://twitter.com/Shellysadventur

Contents

Chapter 1	The Big Day	1
Chapter 2	At the Bank	7
Chapter 3	Opening a Bank Account	12
Chapter 4	Basic Checking and Interest-Bearing Checking Accounts	19
Chapter 5	Sign Me Up	29
Fun Activities		39
What Is a Check?		39
Fill in the Blank		40
Word Search Puzzle		42
Questions and Answers		44
Definition Matching		48
Fill in the Blank		50
Hand Signs		53
Glossary		65
About the Authors		69

Chapter 1

The Big Day

It was Saturday morning, and Shelly was up bright and early. Yesterday was the last day of school and the summer was finally here. She rushed into the living room to find her parents and her brother, KJ, but was surprised to find no one there. Everyone was still asleep.

She looked at the clock. It was only 6:40. No wonder no one was up yet! Shelly was so excited about summer that she had woken up an hour earlier than the usual family wake-up time, between 7:30 and 8:00.

This meant that her family would be up in fifty minutes, or an hour and twenty at the

Shelly Goes to the Bank

latest. Shelly wondered what to do to pass the time. She didn't want to watch cartoons and she wasn't hungry, so she decided to go back to her room and turn on her computer. When she was on her computer, time always went by fast.

She grabbed her pink laptop from the dresser, sat down at the foot of her bed and opened her computer. Now she knew exactly what she wanted to do. She was going to look up information about banking.

Earlier in the week, Shelly's father had told her that he was going to the bank on the weekend to open an account, and he wanted her to come along to interpret for him. Shelly didn't know much about banking, so she decided to look up some information so that she would be prepared before they went.

The first word she entered in the Google search engine was "banking." Many results came up. These were the first seven:

Shelly Goes to the Bank

- ☑ CREDIT CARDS
- ☑ BANK ACCOUNTS, CHECKING AND SAVINGS
- ☑ ONLINE BANKING
- ☑ CHECKING ACCOUNT
- ☑ DEBIT CARDS
- ☑ LOANS
- ☑ RESOURCES

Shelly was a little overwhelmed by all the information on banking. She had thought that banks were just places to save money and that you could take your money out when you needed some. She had no idea that banks did so much more.

She clicked on different links to try to get a better understanding. While she was reading the different pages, she heard the sound of small feet running down the hallway. She knew her baby brother, KJ, was coming, because KJ ran everywhere and every morning he came to Shelly's room as soon as he woke up. He had been doing this since he was old enough to crawl.

KJ ran around the corner into her room and gave her a big hug. Then he used sign language to say "Good morning" and "I love you." She smiled and signed "I love you" back to him. He gave her a big smile and then another hug.

A moment later, their father came to her door. He signed good morning to Shelly and KJ, and both children signed back "Good morning." Shelly's father used sign language to say that he was going to the bank to open a bank account, and they should be ready in twenty minutes. "Get yourselves cleaned up and dressed," he signed.

As KJ ran out of the room, Shelly glanced into the hallway and saw a light flashing

Shelly Goes to the Bank

in the living room. It was the telephone. Whenever the phone rang, a bright light flashed in the living room and her father's room. A bright yellow light flashed when someone was at the front door. Shelly's father had all kinds of gadgets.

Shelly headed to the bathroom to brush her teeth and noticed that her father was talking to someone on his video phone. Shelly was so happy that her father could communicate with people on the phone, even though he was deaf. She got dressed and went to the living room to wait for her father and KJ.

Chapter 2

At the Bank

On the way to the bank Shelly's father stopped the car at Amber's house.

Shelly looked at her father and signed, "Why are we stopping at Amber's house?" Her father signed back to her that he was dropping off KJ. Since her little brother was such a busybody and loved attention, Shelly knew why her dad was leaving him there. He was too young to come to their meeting at the bank.

When Mrs. Maddox and Amber came outside and started walking towards the car, KJ jumped out. He loved going to Amber's house. Usually he cried if he couldn't go somewhere with Shelly and their father, but if he was

Shelly Goes to the Bank

going to Amber's house, he had no problem being left behind. He ran up to Amber and Mrs. Maddox, gave them a big hug and turned around to face the car. "Bye," he signed.

Shelly's father signed to Mrs. Maddox, "Thank you for watching KJ."

She signed back, "No problem, Mr. Martin."

"I wish you could come with us to the bank today," Shelly said to Amber.

"I do, too," said Amber. "When you come back, would you tell me what you learned?"

"Sure thing," said Shelly.

Shelly's dad tapped her shoulder and pointed to the clock, reminding her that they had to go.

"Talk to you later, Amber," Shelly called out as her father backed out of the driveway.

She looked through the back window and saw KJ watching the car until they were almost out of sight. Then she saw him turn and walk towards the house with Amber and Mrs. Maddox.

The bank was only a few minutes' drive

Shelly Goes to the Bank

from Amber's house. When they arrived, the clock on the dashboard blinked 8:15, which meant they were fifteen minutes early. This was perfect for Shelly's father, who always liked to be punctual.

While they waited in the car for the bank to open, he asked her what she wanted to do during the summer. She signed that all she wanted to do was have fun. The answer wasn't good enough for her dad. He signed back that she should think of three things she would like to do. Shelly sat for a few moments, not knowing what to say.

Then she signed back with a smile, "One: I want to go to a theme park with Amber, Maria, and Kasey. Two: I want us to go on a road trip to another state."

Before Shelly could get to number three, her father interrupted her. "Who do you want to go on a road trip with?" he asked.

Shelly signed back, "You, KJ and Bruno." Bruno was the family dog. He understood American Sign Language, too.

"Okay," Shelly's father signed. "What's the third thing?"

She continued. "Three: I want to go to a waterpark. It's going to be a very hot summer. The best thing will be to go swimming in a pool or lake."

Shelly's father smiled, but he didn't sign anything.

"Why are you smiling?" she signed.

"You don't know how to swim," he signed.

"Yes, I can!" she signed. "Remember, I took swimming lessons last summer?"

Shelly's father signed, "Yes, I know." He loved to tease her about things that would get her riled up.

Shelly signed, "Anyways, there are more than three things that I want to do in the summer. I want—"

Her father stopped her, pointing at the clock, which showed that it was time for them to go. Even though the bank would not open for another five minutes, he had seen other cars arriving, and he didn't want to wait

Shelly Goes to the Bank

behind people who had come after them. Shelly hopped out and headed to the main entrance. Her dad grabbed his tote bag from the backseat and glanced inside it to make sure he had all the papers he might need. From the walkway, he could see a woman inside through the big glass windows. She was coming to unlock the doors.

He glanced back and saw two people coming from the cars that had parked nearby. He had gotten out of his car just in time.

The woman opened the door with a smile and said, "Good morning." Reading her lips, he waived and walked into the bank with Shelly.

Chapter 3

Opening a Bank Account

In the bank, Shelly saw three people behind a long counter, waiting for customers. At one end of the room, a woman and a man were sitting at their desks. Shelly thought they must be the bank manager and the assistant bank manager.

Shelly and her father walked past a woman wearing a name badge that said *Lisa*. "How can we help you today?" said Lisa.

Mr. Martin read her lips and signed to Shelly, "Tell Lisa that we are here to open a new bank account." Shelly repeated this to Lisa.

Shelly Goes to the Bank

"Do you know what type of account you want to open?" said Lisa.

Shelly asked her father Lisa's question using sign language. He signed back that he wanted to open a checking account.

Lisa looked at Mr. Martin and said, "Mr. Smith can take care of this for you today at your meeting. I will call you when he is free. Please sign your name on this paper so that I can tell him your name, and take a seat while you wait," she said, pointing to some chairs. She handed Mr. Martin a clipboard with a piece of paper on it, which he signed and gave back to her.

While they waited, Shelly asked her dad what a checking account was. He signed to her, "It's a bank account in which you can deposit money. Then to withdraw it later, you can write a check."

"What's a check?" Shelly signed.

Mr. Martin replied, "A check is a piece of paper on which you can write down a person's name and a certain amount of money. Then

Shelly Goes to the Bank

the person can take the check to the bank and get that amount from your bank account. You can use it to pay for things. I will give you an example. Whenever we go to the store and buy some food, we have to pay for it. We can pay with cash. Another way is to write a check with the exact amount that the food costs and give the check to the shopkeeper. The shopkeeper can take the check to the bank and get the money from our checking account. But in order to write a check, first I have to have a checking account. That is why we came here today."

Shelly interrupted him. "So if you have a check, can you write any amount on it?"

"Oh, no," her dad signed. "Whatever amount you write on the check must already be in your checking account. For example, if the food costs $100 and I pay for it with a check, I must have at least $100 in my checking account."

Just as Shelly was about to ask another question, she saw a man coming towards

Shelly Goes to the Bank

them. "Hello Mr. Martin. Lisa told me you were waiting for me. I am Mr. Smith." The man turned to Shelly and said, "And what is your name?"

"My name is Shelly," she replied.

"Well, hello, Shelly. Nice to meet you," said the banker. "Please come with me."

They followed Mr. Smith to a desk. Shelly and her father took two chairs on one side of the desk and Mr. Smith sat in his chair on the other side.

"Lisa told me that you would like to open a checking account," he said, looking at Shelly's father. Mr. Martin read the banker's lips and nodded his head.

"Well you've come to the right place," said Mr. Smith. "I can definitely help you. Have you ever had an account in our bank?" he asked. Shelly translated to make sure her father understood. Mr. Martin signed, "No, this will be my first account here."

"Well to get started, I need to know what type of checking account you are interested

Shelly Goes to the Bank

in. We have three options." Shelly signed everything to make sure her father understood. Mr. Smith opened a brochure that listed the different types of checking accounts.

1. Basic Checking Account

2. Student Checking Account

3. Interest-bearing Checking Account

Shelly's father took the brochure and crossed off the student checking account. He was not a student, so he knew he would not be allowed to open a student account. The other two types of checking accounts looked similar, so he did not know which one to choose.

He signed, "What's the difference between these two?" Shelly told Mr. Smith what her father wanted to know.

"Those accounts are very similar but they have different benefits and different requirements." Mr. Smith turned around, took some

Shelly Goes to the Bank

forms out of a file cabinet behind his desk and placed the papers in front of Shelly and her father.

Chapter 4

Basic Checking and Interest-Bearing Checking Accounts

Mr. Smith laid out the papers on the desk so Shelly and Mr. Martin could see them while he explained the differences between the two kinds of checking accounts. He said, "Mr. Martin, a Basic Checking Account would give you two main benefits:

Shelly Goes to the Bank

1. You will get a debit card. You can use a debit card in regular stores and in online stores to pay for things you want to buy.

2. You can pay bills online. This means you will be able to pay bills such as electricity and phone bills directly by logging into your checking account online.

Mr. Smith added, "This type of checking account has a maintenance fee."

Shelly translated what Mr. Smith had said into sign language. Mr. Martin signed to her, "What is a maintenance fee? How much does it cost?" and Shelly asked the banker.

Mr. Smith replied, "A maintenance fee is what the bank charges you, the customer, to have the account. The fee for the Basic Checking Account is $10 per month but there is a way that you can avoid having to pay this fee." He placed another brochure in front of

Shelly Goes to the Bank

them, pointed to it and said, "This shows two ways that you can avoid having to pay the monthly maintenance fee:

1. Set up a direct deposit of $200 into the checking account every month. I can arrange this for you if you wish.

2. Maintain a balance of at least $1,000 all the time."

Shelly was puzzled. "What is a direct deposit?" she asked.

Mr. Smith replied, "Instead of depositing money into your checking account once in a while, a direct deposit is an automatic transfer of money into your account on a regular schedule. For example, if Mr. Smith has a job, he can ask his employer to deposit his salary directly into his checking account every week or every month. If the boss pays you every Friday morning, then every Friday when you wake up, you will see that the

Shelly Goes to the Bank

amount has been deposited in your account automatically."

"That's cool," Shelly said. What's the difference between the Basic Checking Account and the Interest-bearing Checking Account?"

Mr. Smith replied, "The Interest-bearing Checking Account has all the same benefits as the Basic Checking Account plus more. He placed another paper in front of Mr. Martin and Shelly and read out the extra benefits:

- ☑ THE OPTION TO ADD UP TO 5 SAVINGS ACCOUNTS TO THE MAIN ACCOUNT

- ☑ NO FEES FOR WIRE TRANSFERS

"I think I should explain wire transfers," he said. "A wire transfer lets you move money from one bank account to another electronically. For example, if you wanted to send money to someone, you could transfer it directly from your bank account to their bank

Shelly Goes to the Bank

account without having to take the money out of the bank."

"If I have my own account, can my dad transfer money from his bank account to mine?" Shelly asked with a big smile.

"Yes. Exactly!" said Mr. Smith "You're never too young to have a bank account. Actually, a savings account is the best kind of bank account for kids because it helps them start saving money at a young age. After your father opens his checking account, I'll tell you all about our savings accounts."

Shelly had never heard of a kid having a bank account. She got excited at the thought of having one because it would help her save lots of money.

She turned to her father and signed, "Dad, I would like to have a bank account."

Mr. Martin signed back, "Wait. Let me decide which checking account I am going to open for myself."

Mr. Smith continued to tell Shelly and her father the rest of the benefits of the

Interest-bearing Checking Account. He said, "This type of account also has

- ☑ OVERDRAFT PROTECTION FROM YOUR SAVINGS ACCOUNT WITH NO FEES

- ☑ INTEREST PAYMENTS ON THE MONEY THAT YOU HAVE IN THE ACCOUNT.

"The regular checking account that I mentioned earlier has a fee for overdraft protection, but this one gives it to you for free," he explained.

"What is overdraft protection?" Shelly asked.

"Overdraft protection is a service offered by the bank that allows a person with a checking account to buy something even if they don't have sufficient funds in their bank account to cover the cost. But of course, the person has to get the money to pay for the purchase from somewhere else. If you have

Shelly Goes to the Bank

this type of checking account, the bank automatically moves money from your backup funding source into your checking account to cover the purchase or to pay a bill," Mr. Smith explained.

"I will give you an example," he continued. "If you go to the store and purchase a hat for $10 with your debit card or a check and you only have $7 in your checking account, your account would be three dollars short. In banking terms, you would have an overdraft of three dollars. But if you have overdraft protection, the bank will automatically transfer three dollars from your savings account into your checking account to cover the overdraft for you, so that you can pay for your purchase."

"But what if we don't have any money in our savings account?" Shelly asked.

"If you don't have any money in your savings account, you'll be charged an overdraft fee by the bank of $35."

Shelly's eyes opened wide. "Wow! Thirty-five dollars?" she said. "That's a lot of money."

"Yes, it is. That's why it's important to always be aware of how much money you have in your bank account," said Mr. Smith. "That's also why overdraft protection is a good benefit to have."

Shelly's father had been reading Mr. Smith's lips all along, but Shelly repeated what he had said in sign language anyway.

Mr. Martin signed, "Can you tell me about the interest that I would earn with this account?" and Shelly repeated the question out loud.

Mr. Smith explained, "If you have $50,000 or less in your Interest-bearing Checking Account, you will get 2% interest on your balance every month. If you have between $50,000 and $100,000 you will get 3% on your balance each month. And if you have over $100,000 you will get 4%.

"What are the fees for this type of account?" Shelly's father signed.

Mr. Smith replied, "There is no fee as long as you keep a balance of $10,000 or more in the account." Shelly was shocked to hear such a high number.

After hearing that answer, Mr. Martin signed to Shelly that he knew which kind of checking account he wanted.

Chapter 5

Sign Me Up

"Which kind of account do you think would be best for you, Mr. Martin?" Mr. Smith asked. "We can open the account today." Shelly signed the question to her father.

Mr. Martin knew he wouldn't be able to keep $10,000 in his account at all times because he did not have enough income, so he decided to open a Basic Checking Account. It would be easy for him to maintain and it would be a good starter account. Mr. Martin pointed to the piece of paper with the title, "Basic Checking Account."

"Excellent choice!" said Mr. Smith. "Now that you've picked the checking account you want to open, let me tell you a little bit about the different types of saving accounts that you can pair up with your checking account. We currently offer three different savings accounts to help you meet your needs. They are all very similar, with just a few differences. These are the three options that we offer:

- ☑ REGULAR SAVINGS ACCOUNT
- ☑ CUSTODIAL SAVINGS ACCOUNT
- ☑ MONEY MARKET SAVINGS ACCOUNT

"The Custodial Savings Account and the Regular Savings Account have the same fees and interest rates. The Custodial Savings Account is good if you want to save for your child's future. For both accounts, you have to maintain the same minimum balance. The

Shelly Goes to the Bank

Regular Savings Account works well with a Basic Checking Account because they can be linked."

"What are linked accounts?" Shelly asked.

Mr. Smith explained, "You can login on-line and see all your linked accounts at the same time. You can also easily transfer money from any account that is linked to any other account."

"You said that a minimum balance must be maintained in the savings account at all times. How much is that?" Shelly asked.

"For both the Custodial Savings Account and the Regular Savings Account, the minimum balance required is only $20," Mr. Smith replied. "And if you open one type or both today, you'll be able to do so for free, because we are running a great promotion. We will give our customers $250 for every new savings account this month."

"*Whaaat?*" Shelly yelled. "Are you saying that if my father opens an account for me today, the bank will give me $250 dollars?"

Mr. Smith laughed aloud. "Yes, exactly," he said, leaning back in his chair.

Mr. Martin didn't understand everything Mr. Smith was saying, so when he saw Shelly getting excited, he asked her what was happening. Shelly apologized for not telling him right away and signed what Mr. Smith had said. Mr. Martin gave her a big smile.

"That sounds great!" he signed.

"What are the advantages of the other kind of account?" Shelly asked the banker.

Mr. Smith said, "The Money Market Savings Account has the same minimum opening deposit as the other two, which is $20. This means that when you open your savings account, you have to put $20 into it. But there are two big differences between the Money Market Savings Account and the others. First, it gives a higher interest rate, but the monthly balance that you have to maintain is $2500, which is much higher. Second, the monthly fee is $12, and for the other two kinds of savings accounts it is only $4."

Shelly Goes to the Bank

The banker looked at Shelly's father and said, "I think the Basic Savings Account would be a good way for you to start if you are only opening an account for yourself, Mr. Martin. But if you would also like to open a savings account for Shelly, the Custodial Savings Account would be best. Remember, you can change later if you wish, anytime. You don't have to stick with the kind of account you open today. We have other types of bank accounts, but to get started, these are what I recommend."

Shelly explained to her father what Mr. Smith had said, and he signed that he agreed with the recommendation. He decided to open the Custodial Savings Account. Shelly was happy that she would have her own bank account.

Mr. Smith was happy that new customers were opening accounts at his bank. He said he would be back in a moment and left the room. When he returned he had some new booklets and papers and placed them on the desk in front of Mr. Martin.

Shelly Goes to the Bank

"Mr. Martin," said the banker, "this is an information booklet that tells you everything you need to know about your bank accounts and online access to them. Whenever you wish, you will be able to go online to view your account balance and see the other services that the bank offers."

Mr. Smith handed Shelly's father a smaller booklet and said, "These are some blank checks for your checking account," he said. "You can use them anytime. One of the pages tells you how to order more checks when you need them."

He gave Mr. Martin one more item. "This is a check register booklet. If you fill it out whenever you write a check or make a deposit into your account, you can keep track of your spending and see how much money you have at all times."

While Mr. Smith explained the details, Shelly signed everything to her dad to make sure he understood.

Mr. Smith handed Mr. Martin a bank card.

Shelly Goes to the Bank

"This is your temporary debit card," said the banker. "We will send the official card in the mail, and you will receive it in about ten business days." He put a small machine with a number pad on the desk in front of Shelly's father and continued, "Now, please enter your private four-digit pass code on the number pad. This will be your personal code or password for the debit card. You must keep this code a secret."

Shelly explained everything to her father. Mr. Martin entered his code on the number pad.

"Please enter it once more," said Mr. Smith.

Mr. Martin entered his personal code again.

"You're all set! You and Shelly now have bank accounts. The $250 bonus will be deposited into Shelly's savings account on Monday morning."

Shelly was so happy! She now had her own bank account.

Everyone stood up, and Mr. Smith reached out to shake Mr. Martin's hand. "Thank you

Shelly Goes to the Bank

for your business today, Mr. Martin," he said. "We're happy to welcome you as a new customer." He reached into his pocket for his business card and handed it to Mr. Martin. The card had Mr. Smith's name and phone number. It also had a phone number marked especially for the "Deaf and Hard of Hearing."

"If you need anything, please don't hesitate to call me," Mr. Smith said. "The bank has other products that might be worthwhile for you, and I'd be happy to tell you about them."

Mr. Martin nodded his head and signed, "Thank you for your help."

Mr. Smith signed back, "You're welcome."

Shelly and her father looked at each other in surprise.

Mr. Smith laughed with delight and signed, "Nice to meet you."

Shelly and Mr. Martin smiled and signed back, "Nice to meet you, too."

As they got in the car and drove off, Shelly thought, "This is going to be a great summer!"

Fun Activities

What Is a Check?

Routing, Account Number,
Check Number, Name, Bank Name,
Pay to the Order of, Amount

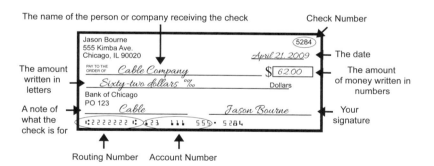

Shelly Goes to the Bank

Fill in the Blank

EXAMPLE 1:

1. Where is the Routing Number?
2. Where is the Account Number?
3. What is his/her name?
4. What is their address?
5. What amount is he/she writing the check for?
6. What are they writing the check for?
7. What date did they write the check?

LYDIA, Inc.
3000 Calle Quieta
Santa Fe, NM 87507
1025
DATE *4/13/2015*

PAY TO THE ORDER OF *Santa Fe City* $ *1298.62*
One thousand two hundred ninety-eight 62/100   DOLLARS

MEMO *Rent*   *Lydia, Inc.*
⑈000000000⑈ ⑈000000000⑈   1025

Shelly Goes to the Bank

Example 2:

Write out a check to Shelly's Adventures in the amount of $13 for the hardcover book, *Shelly Goes to the Zoo.*

Shelly Goes to the Bank

Word Search Puzzle

CHECKING

SAVINGS

CHECK

BILL

DEPOSIT

WITHDRAWAL

FEE

OVERDRAFT

DEBIT

CREDIT

ACCOUNT

STATEMENT

Shelly Goes to the Bank

```
U R N V Y V E J P Y K T L Y I
C L X H I U M A R Y E E F R S
Y C P F N J I I E B D J W A W
F J D S O B I L L F V G B G H
X F H Z E V A J R R R D Y B B
M E M M Y L W D I A E N T G O
D W N J V O C J S P S D Z F N
Z A T C S Y R V O P F D R N I
P D E C D B T S V Y S D R I Q
M N L M N P I L A Y E P Z O N
X S H N D T G E I V C M F S J
S O H V S F A W H H H P P R L
D T B X R Y B K E Z B H G T J
T D U M T N X C R E D I T A K
F X O K W F K Z J F W X I G Z
A A Q F U I A L K O S O B E T
A C S N N H T R D S Y L E V N
C L W G D S X H D G M Y D F E
C Z T K N M C W D R O R B P M
O V E S V I X Z G R E C D X E
U G N G J C V Q D Q A V V F T
N T E V T H M A L R K W O F A
T M Z F O E J U S N Y I A W T
N S G J T C C D V Z D Q C L S
A H J Z S K S K G V G K Y H F
```

Questions and Answers

Chapter 1:

1. Why was Shelly's father going to the bank?
2. Why was Shelly overwhelmed by all the information she found online about banking?
3. Why did Shelly's father and brother use sign language?

Chapter 2:

1. What time did the bank open?
2. Who is Bruno and what makes him unique?
3. Name two things Shelly looked forward to doing during Summer vacation.

Chapter 3:

1. What example did Dad use to describe how to pay for items with a check?

2. Name two types of checking accounts.
3. Why couldn't Shelly's father open a student checking account?

Chapter 4:

1. Describe a key benefit of a basic checking account.
2. Describe a key benefit of an interest-bearing checking account.
3. What type of bank account did the bank recommend for Shelly?

Chapter 5:

1. Which type of checking account did Shelly's father choose?
2. Name two types of savings accounts.
3. How much did the bank deposit into Shelly's account?

Shelly Goes to the Bank

KEY:

CHAPTER 1: 1. To open an account. 2. She initially thought that banks were just places to save, deposit and withdraw money when needed. 3. They are deaf.

CHAPTER 2: 1. 8:30 a.m. 2. The family dog that uses ASL to communicate. 3. Visit a theme park, visit a waterpark, take a road trip out of state.

CHAPTER 3: 1. A trip to the grocery store. 2. Basic, student, interest-bearing. 3. He is not a student.

CHAPTER 4: 1. Debit card, online bill pay. 2. Option to add up to five savings accounts to the main account, fee-free wire transfers, overdraft protection. 3. Savings account.

CHAPTER 5: 1. Basic checking account. 2. Regular, custodial, money market. 3. $250.

Shelly Goes to the Bank

Shelly Goes to the Bank

Definition Matching

- ☐ a print or online document that displays all your account transactions for a specific time frame
- ☐ a check that is returned to the depositor due to insufficient funds in the account
- ☐ a check that is issued by a bank and paid from its funds
- ☐ a card that can be used to withdraw cash at an ATM or make purchases
- ☐ money added into a customer's bank account
- ☐ money removed from a customer's bank account
- ☐ an account owned by two or more people
- ☐ a deposit account that prohibits withdrawal by check
- ☐ a fee assessed when an item is declined and returned unpaid due to insufficient funds
- ☐ a fee assessed when an item is authorized and paid due to insufficient funds

Shelly Goes to the Bank

- NSF fee
- regular savings account
- account statement
- deposit
- bounced check
- joint account
- cashier's check
- overdraft fee
- check card
- withdrawal

Shelly Goes to the Bank

Fill in the Blank

1. A _____ is a bank account in which you can deposit and withdraw money.

2. A _____ is a piece of paper on which you can write down a person's name and a certain amount of money.

3. _____ is a service that lets you pay your bills online.

4. A _____ is an automatic transfer of money into your account on a regular schedule.

5. A _____ is an amount the bank charges you to have an account.

6. A _____ enables you to move money from one bank account to another electronically.

Shelly Goes to the Bank

7. _____ links your checking account to another bank account to transfer funds and prevent transactions from being declined.

8. A _____ can be used to withdraw cash at an ATM or make purchases.

9. A _____ allows consumers to make purchases on credit.

10. A _____ is a savings account that offers a higher interest rate than a regular savings account.

Key:

1. checking account 2. check 3. bill pay 4. direct deposit 5. maintenance fee 6. wire transfer 7. overdraft protection 8. debit card 9. credit card 10. money market savings account

Hand Signs

On the following pages,
Kasey demonstrates 10 signs for
basketball terms and other frequently
used words used in this story.

Visit the Shelly's Adventures
YouTube page at
https://youtube.com/user/ShellysAdventuresLLC
for an interactive tutorial.

Shelly Goes to the Bank

TRANSFER

Move your hand from one area to another area.

Shelly Goes to the Bank

DOLLAR

Slide your top hand over your other hand.

Shelly Goes to the Bank

PAY

Flick the hand that is pointed outward.

Shelly Goes to the Bank

Swipe hand as if you are snatching money.

Shelly Goes to the Bank

BUSINESS

Move the hand with the b-shape back and forth.

Shelly Goes to the Bank

SAVE

Tap the back of the hand with the two fingers.

Shelly Goes to the Bank

CARD

Make the shape of a card.

Shelly Goes to the Bank

MONEY

Tap your hand twice in the palm of the other hand.

Shelly Goes to the Bank

THOUSAND

Move your other hand into the middle of the other hand.

Shelly Goes to the Bank

DEPOSIT

Push both thumbs
out and then down.

Shelly Goes to the Bank

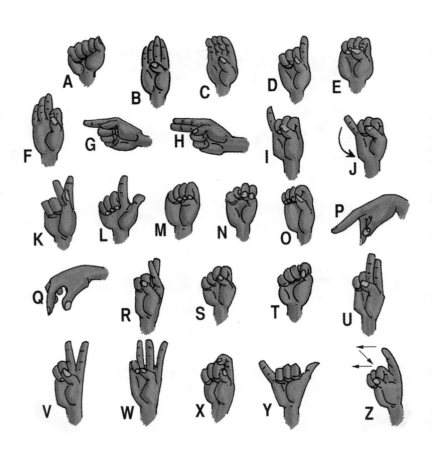

Glossary

A

Account statement: a print or online document that displays all your account transactions for a specified time frame

B

Bill Pay: a service that lets you pay your bills online

Bounced check: a check that is returned to the depositor due to insufficient funds in the account

C

Cashier's check: a check that is issued and paid by bank funds

Check: a piece of paper on which you can write down a person's name and a certain amount of money

Checking account: a bank account in which you can deposit and withdraw money

Check card (or debit card): a card that can be used to withdraw cash at an ATM or make purchases

Credit card: a card that allows consumers to make purchases on credit

Custodial account: An account created for the benefit of a minor (a person under the age of 18 or 21 depending on state law) with an adult as the account's custodian.

D

Deposit: money added into a customer's bank

Direct deposit: an automatic transfer of money into your account on a regular schedule

Shelly Goes to the Bank

Disclosure: Information pertaining to an account's services, fees and regulatory requirements.

J

Joint account: an account owned by two or more people

M

Maintenance fee: an amount the bank charges you to have an account

Money market savings account: a savings account that offers a higher interest rate than a regular savings account

N

NSF fee: a fee assessed when an item is declined and returned unpaid due to insufficient funds

O

Overdraft fee: a fee assessed when an item is authorized and paid due to insufficient funds

Overdraft protection: links your checking account to another bank account to transfer funds and prevent transactions from being declined

R

Regular Savings account: a deposit account that prohibits withdrawal by check

W

Wire transfer: enables you to move money from one bank account to another electronically

Withdrawal: money removed from a customer's bank account

About the Authors

ALLISON MARTIN is a personal finance expert and journalist. She also holds undergraduate and graduate degrees in accounting from the University of South Florida.

Her work has been featured on The Wall Street Journal, ABC News, MSN Money, Yahoo! Finance, Fox Business, CentSai, Investopedia, Credit.com and MoneyTalks News. She also travels around the U.S. hosting financial literacy and entrepreneurship workshops to individuals from all walks of life.

When she's not busy writing, Allison enjoys and mentoring mommy-preneurs through her consulting firm, Mommy Commander, traveling and spending time with her family.

KENTRELL MARTIN is the creator of the Shelly's Adventures Series. He has written over 20 books and is looking forward to turning the Shelly's Adventures Series into a cartoon series and live action show in the near future. He holds an undergraduate degree in business management from the University of New Orleans.

Kentrell travels across the country visiting schools and teaching American Sign Language. He visits over 120 schools per year and has a goal of eventually visiting 200 schools in a year. In the next year, Kentrell plans to take school visits abroad.

When he's not busy thinking of the next adventure in the Shelly's Adventures Series, Kentrell enjoys playing basketball, spending time with his family, and traveling.

Shelly's Adventures Books

Current Titles

Shelly Goes to the Zoo *(picture book)*
Shelly's Outdoor Adventure *(picture book)*
Kasey's First Day of Basketball Practice
(chapter book, co-authored with Kentrell Martin Jr.)

Future Titles

Picture Books

Basketball 101 with Kasey
Shelly Babysits Her Baby Brother
Shelly Goes to the Dentist
Maria Goes to the Fiesta
KJ's Emotional Day
KJ's First Sight Words
Shelly Visits Washington, D.C.

Chapter Books

Kasey's First Day of Football Practice
Kasey's First Day of Baseball Practice
Shelly's Adventures—Christmas Break
Shelly and KJ Learn to Work Together
Amber Meets a New Friend